First American Edition 2003 by
Kane/Miller Book Publishers, Inc.
La Jolla, California

Original title: Selma
Copyright © 2002 by Jutta Bauer/Lappan
Verlag GmbH, D-26121 Oldenburg, Germany

For more information contact:
Kane/Miller Book Publishers
P.O. Box 8515
La Jolla, CA 92038
www.kanemiller.com

Library of Congress Control Number: 2002117378
Printed and bound in Singapore

1   2   3   4   5   6   7   8   9   10

ISBN 1-929132-50-6

JUTTA BAUER

Selma

Kane/Miller
BOOK PUBLISHERS

When I just couldn't take it anymore,
I went to the wise ram...

Once there was a sheep named Selma...

Every morning at sunrise,
Selma would eat a little grass...

...she would play with her children
until lunchtime...

...exercise in the afternoon...

...eat some more grass...

...have a little chat with Mrs. Miller
in the evening...

...and finally, fall fast asleep.

Asked what she would do if she had more time, Selma replied...

Well, I would eat a little grass at sunrise...

...play with my children until lunchtime...

...exercise in the afternoon...

...eat some more grass...

...have a little chat with
Mrs. Miller in the evening...

...and finally, fall fast asleep.

"And if you won a million dollars?"
she was asked.

Well, I would love
to eat a little grass in the morning...

...play with my children...

...exercise in the afternoon...

...eat some more grass...

..and it would be nice to have a chat
with Mrs. Miller in the evening...

...before finally, falling
fast asleep.